HOW TO DRAW
MANGA

David Antram

Hatch

First published in the UK in 2010 by The Salariya Book Company Ltd
This edition published in the UK in 2024 by Hatch Press,
an imprint of Bonnier Books UK
4th Floor, Victoria House
Bloomsbury Square, London WC1B 4DA
Owned by Bonnier Books
Sveavägen 56, Stockholm, Sweden
www.bonnierbooks.co.uk

Copyright © 2024 by Hatch Press

1 3 5 7 9 10 8 6 4 2

All rights reserved

ISBN 978-1-80078-768-1

Printed in China

Contents

4 .... Making a start
6 .... Drawing tools
8 .... Materials
10 .... Perspective
12 .... Heads
14 .... Expressions
16 .... Hair
18 .... Samurai
20 .... Martial arts
22 .... Warrior
24 .... Robot
26 .... Kimono girl
28 .... Explosive action!
30 .... Robo-tortoise and girl
32 .... Glossary and Index

Making a start

Learning to draw is about looking and seeing. Keep practising and get to know your subject. Use a sketchbook to make quick sketches. Start by doodling and experimenting with shapes and patterns. There are many ways to draw; this book shows one method. Visit art galleries, look at artists' drawings, see how friends draw, but above all, find your own way.

Use simple shapes to draw the figure in action.

Drawing tools

Here are just a few of the many tools that you can use for drawing. Let your imagination go, and have fun experimenting with all the different marks you can make.

Each grade of **pencil** makes a different mark, from fine, grey lines through to soft, black ones. Hard pencils are graded as H, 2H, 3H, 4H, 5H and 6H (the hardest). A HB pencil is ideal for general sketching. Soft pencils are graded from B, 2B, 3B, 4B, 5B to 6B (the softest and blackest).

Watercolour pencils come in many different colours and make a line similar to a HB pencil. But paint over your finished drawing with clean water and the lines will soften and run.

It is less messy and easier to achieve a fine line with a **charcoal pencil** than a stick of charcoal. Create soft tones by smudging lines with your finger. Ask an adult to spray the drawing with fixative to prevent further smudging.

Pastels are brittle sticks of powdered colour. They blend and smudge easily and are ideal for quick sketches. Pastel drawings work well on textured, coloured paper. Ask an adult to spray your finished drawing with fixative.

Experiment with finger painting. Your fingerprints make exciting patterns and textures. Use your fingers to smudge soft pencil, charcoal and pastel lines.

Ballpoint pens are very useful for sketching and making notes. Make different tones by building up layers of shading.

A mapping pen has to be dipped into bottled ink to fill the nib. Different nib shapes make different marks. Try putting a diluted ink wash over parts of the finished drawing.

Draughtsman's pens and specialist art pens can produce extremely fine lines and are ideal for creating surface texture. A variety of pen nibs are available which produce different widths of line.

Felt-tip pens are ideal for quick sketches. If the ink is not waterproof, try drawing on wet paper and see what happens.

Broad-nibbed marker pens make interesting lines and are good for large, bold sketches. Use a black pen for the main sketch and a grey one to block in areas of shadow.

Paintbrushes are shaped differently to make different marks. Japanese brushes are soft and produce beautiful flowing lines. Large sable brushes are good for painting a wash over a line drawing. Fine brushes are good for drawing delicate lines.

Materials

Try using different types of drawing papers and materials. Experiment with charcoal, wax crayons and pastels. All pens, from felt-tips to ballpoints, will make interesting marks. Try drawing with pen and ink on wet paper.

Ink silhouette

Felt-tips come in a range of line widths. The wider pens are good for filling in large areas of flat tone.

Silhouette is a style of drawing which mainly uses solid black shapes.

Pencil drawings can include a vast amount of detail and tone. Try experimenting with the different grades of pencil to get a range of light and shade effects in your drawing.

Remember, the best equipment and materials will not necessarily make the best drawing - only practice will!

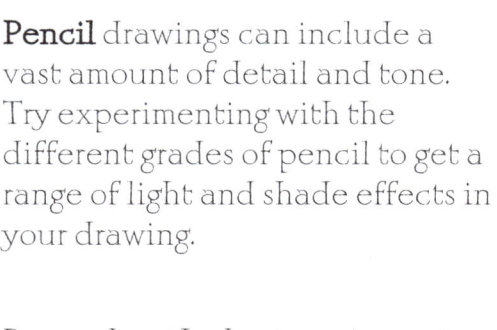

Lines drawn in **ink** cannot be erased, so keep your ink drawings sketchy and less rigid. Don't worry about mistakes, as these can be lost in the drawing as it develops.

It can be tricky adding light and shade to a drawing with a pen. Use a solid layer of ink for the very darkest areas and cross-hatching (straight lines criss-crossing each other) for ordinary dark tones. Hatching (straight lines running parallel to each other) can be used for midtones.

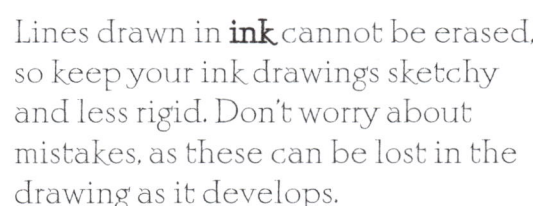

Hatching

Cross-hatching

Perspective

If you look at any object from different viewpoints, you will see that the part that is closest to you looks larger, and the part furthest away from you looks smaller. Drawing in perspective is a way of creating a feeling of space – of showing three dimensions on a flat surface.

The vanishing point (V.P.) is the place in a perspective drawing where parallel lines appear to meet. The position of the vanishing point depends on the viewer's eye level. Sometimes a low viewpoint can give your drawing added drama.

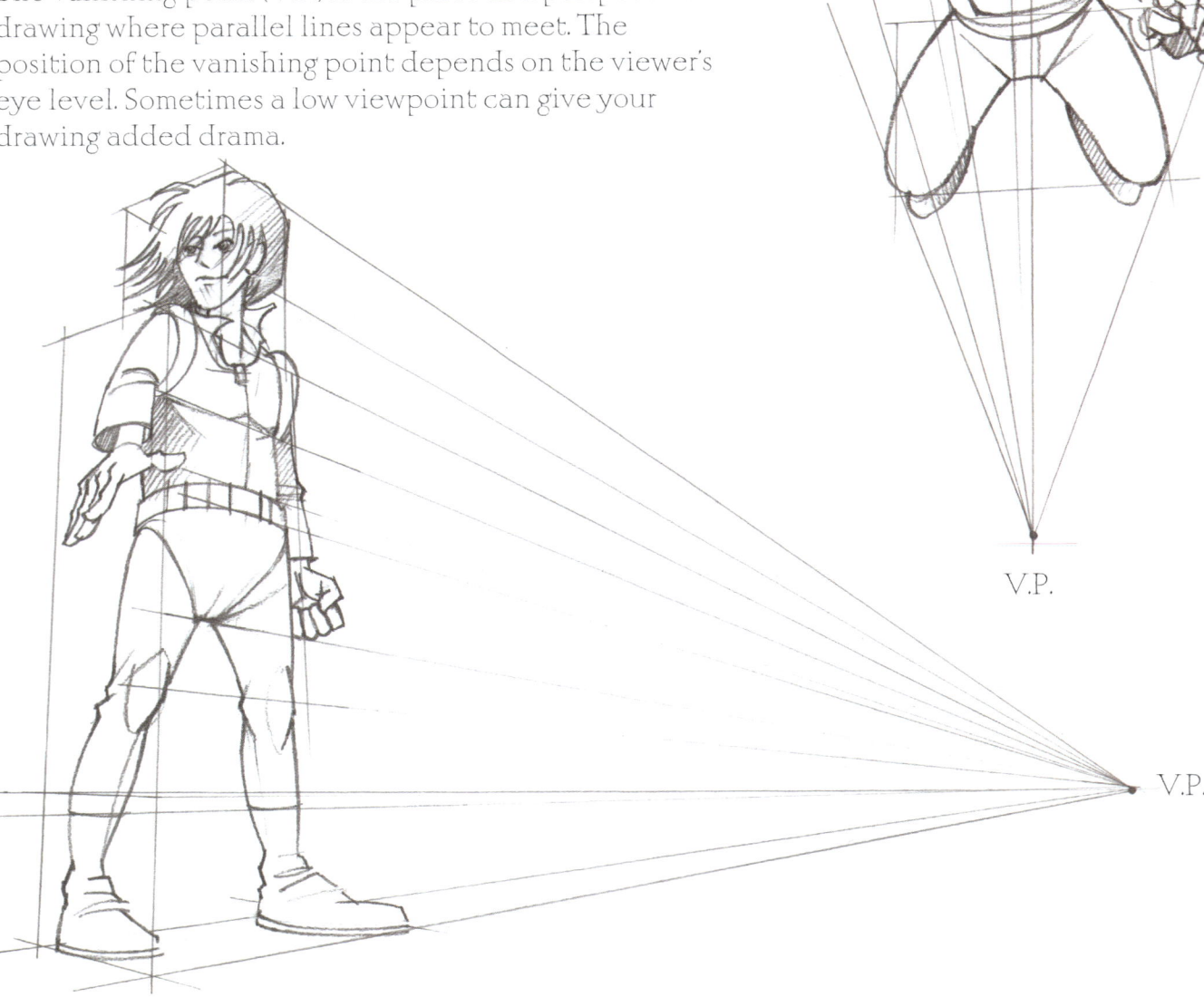

V.P.

V.P.

Two-point perspective drawing

Low eye level
(view from below)

Two-point perspective uses two vanishing points: one for lines running along the length of the object, and one on the opposite side for lines running across the width of the object.

Normal eye level

High eye level
(view from above)

V.P. = vanishing point

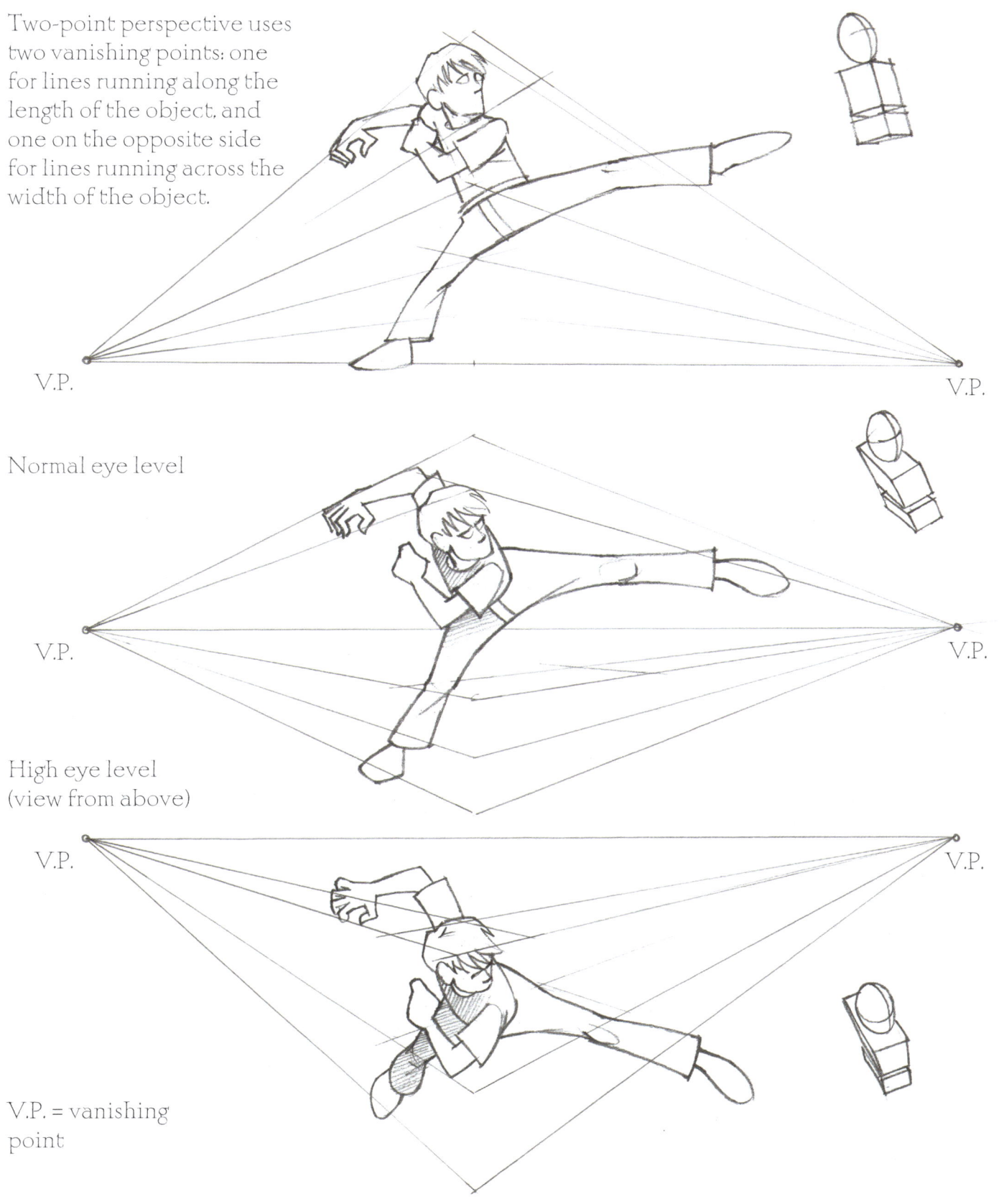

Heads

Manga heads have a distinct style and shape. This is the basic shape of a head from the side and front views.

A simple side view of a head:

Start with a box to help you to proportion your drawing.

Draw an oval in the top two thirds of the box.

Add a line halfway up the box for the eye level.

Add the ear near the centre of the box.

Sketch in a triangle shape for the chin.

Add a triangle shape for the eye.

Draw in the profile of the nose and mouth.

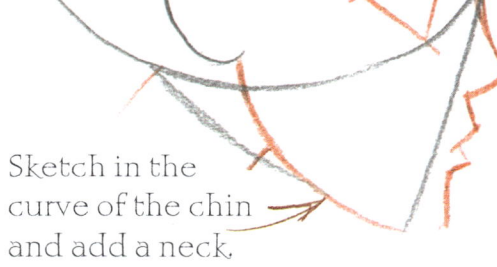

Sketch in the curve of the chin and add a neck.

Draw in the arched eyebrows.

Add on the jagged shaped hair.

Add simple detail to the ear.

Complete the definition of the profile.

Finish any facial details.

A simple front view of a head:

First draw a large oval for the face. Draw two lines dividing the face horizontally and vertically through its centre. Add two small ovals on the horizontal line for the eyes.

On the vertical line mark in the position of the bottom of the nose and the mouth. Draw in the eyebrows. Add ears to the outside of the oval. Make the chin more angular by drawing a curved line from each ear to the centre of the oval.

Draw in the oversized shape of the eyes. Add the small nose and mouth. Draw in the hair using jagged lines and add shading to the eyes. Finish off by carefully removing the construction lines.

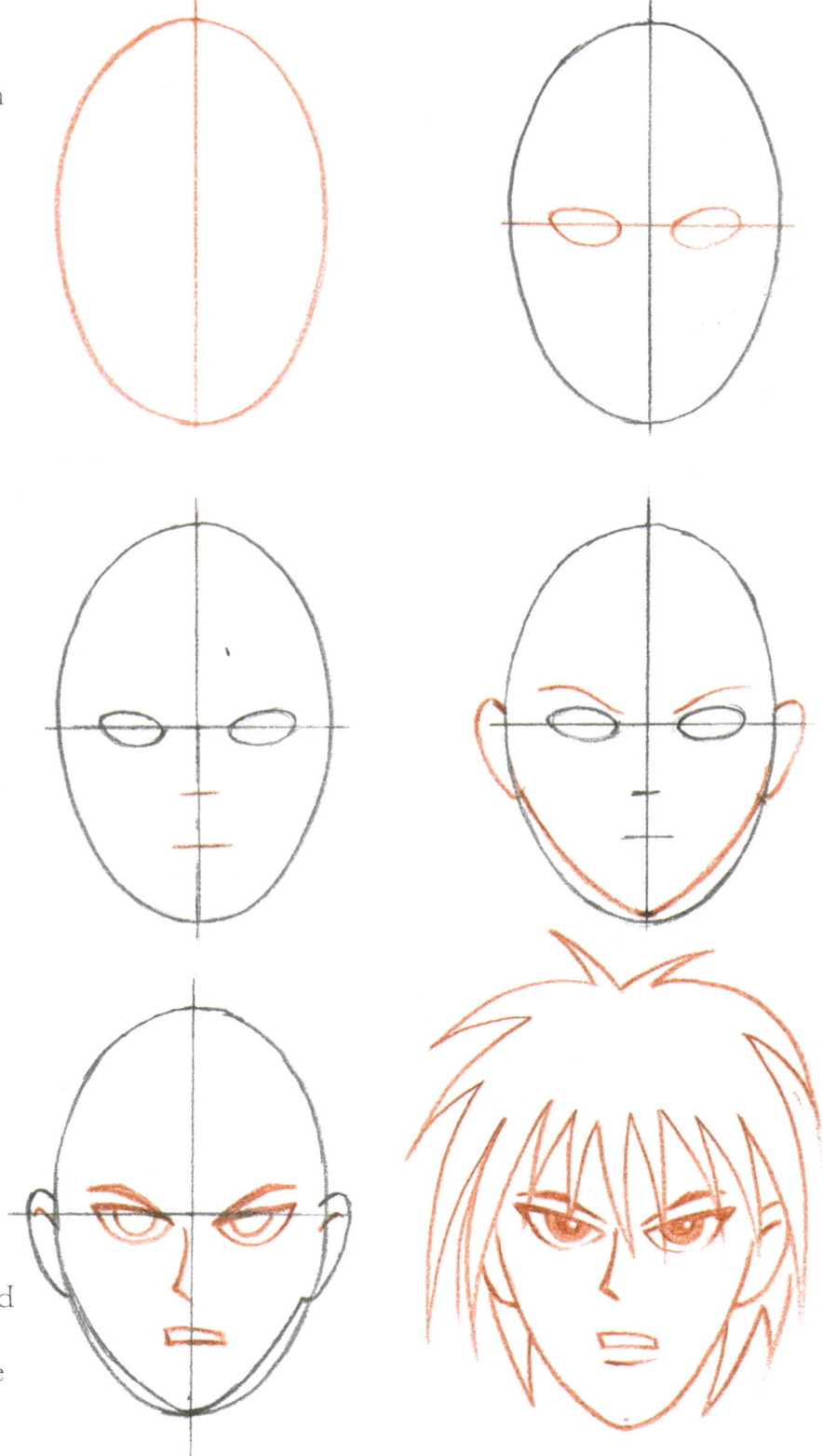

13

Expressions

Drawing different facial expressions is very important in manga. It's the way to show instantly what your character is thinking or feeling. Try drawing facial expressions.

Using a mirror

Look at your own face in the mirror. By pulling different expressions you will see how to draw these in your cartoons.

Start by drawing an oval shape. Make it three dimensional with curved lines going through the centre.

Use these construction lines to add the basic details of the head (see page 13).

Add the mouth, eyebrows and shape of the nose.

Finish the drawing by adding hair and facial details, making the person look happy.

Now try drawing some different expressions.
Here are a few ideas to get you started.

Laughing

Angry

Annoyed

Shocked

Surprised

Shouting

Hair

Manga characters generally have very stylised hair. Think about the situation the character you are drawing is in and make the hair fit the scene.

This character is drawn with five different hair situations.

Hair can be affected by action or environment. For example, if the character is running their hair may stream out behind them, or if it is windy the hair can be blown sideways.

Hair styles can help define your character's personality. Here are a few different styles to try.

17

Samurai

The samurai warrior stands defiant, sword drawn and ready for battle.

Now start to build up the basic shape and features of your figure.

Draw in the main shape of the body using the ovals to guide you.

Start by sketching these simple shapes.

Draw an oval for the head.

Draw an oval for the body and smaller ovals for the hands.

Draw two lines to indicate the position and angle of the shoulders and hips. Draw in a line for the spine.

Draw an oval for the hips.

Sketch in the arms and legs using straight lines. Add dots to indicate the joints.

Indicate the direction and length of the sword.

Sketch in simple shapes for the feet.

Draw in simple tube shapes for the arms and legs.

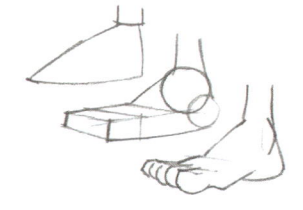

Drawing feet

These drawings show how the foot is built up from a simple shape to its finished form.

Now take your figure a stage further.

Add details to the head, defining the nose, eyes, ears and hair.

Start sketching in the samurai's robes using straight lines.

Complete the details of the face and hair.

Add a tied sash to the front of the robe.

Draw in the shape of the sword.

Add the sword scabbard.

Add shading to define the folds in the robe.

Complete the sword with single sharp lines.

Finish the samurai's scabbard.

Start to build up the shape of the feet.

Finish the details of the feet, adding sandals.

Carefully rub out any unwanted construction lines that remain.

Martial arts

Manga figures are often shown in action, performing martial arts moves.

Sketch an oval for the head.

Draw two lines to indicate the position and angle of the shoulders and hips. Draw in a line for the spine.

Draw triangle shapes to position the feet.

Draw the limbs with straight lines.

Add an overlapping oval for the body and another for the hips.

Indicate the joints with dots.

Sketch in the position of the facial features.

Add circles for the joints.

Using your construction lines as a guide, sketch the simple tube shapes for the arms and legs.

Draw in the shape of the clothes, making sure that they go around the body and flare out at the end of the limbs.

Add spiky hair and start to finish the face.

Draw in the shape of the fingers.

Draw the toes on the feet.

Complete the feet and ankles.

Draw a necklace swinging around the character's neck to add a sense of movement.

Complete the facial features.

Add shading and tone to the clothes.

Add creases to the cloth.

Dynamic backgrounds

A dynamic background can give your drawing more impact. Try drawing straight lines coming out from the figure to give this kick more kick!

21

Warrior

This warrior is rushing into battle wielding a club. His action pose and sense of movement create a dynamic drawing.

Draw in different sized ovals for the head, body, hands and hips.

Draw in a line to place the club.

Draw limbs with straight lines.

Only draw in one line for this leg because it is only the thigh that is visible in this pose.

Indicate the joints with dots.

Sketch in the club.

Using the construction lines as a guide, start drawing in the main shapes of the body.

Draw in circles for the joints.

Draw in tube shapes for the legs. Remember that this pose will effect the leg length.

Draw in square shapes for the clenched fists.

22

Robot

This robot is built in a humanoid form and is ready to perform whatever task it is set.

Draw different sized ovals for the head, body and hips.

Add the visor of the robot's head.

Add the neck.

Sketch in oval shapes for the hands.

Draw two lines to indicate the position and angle of the shoulders and hips. Draw in a line for the spine.

Draw simple lines for the limbs, adding dots at the joints.

Start sketching in the robot's mechanical fingers.

Sketch in the shape of the arms and legs, adding circles for both elbows and knees.

Sketch in the shape of the feet.

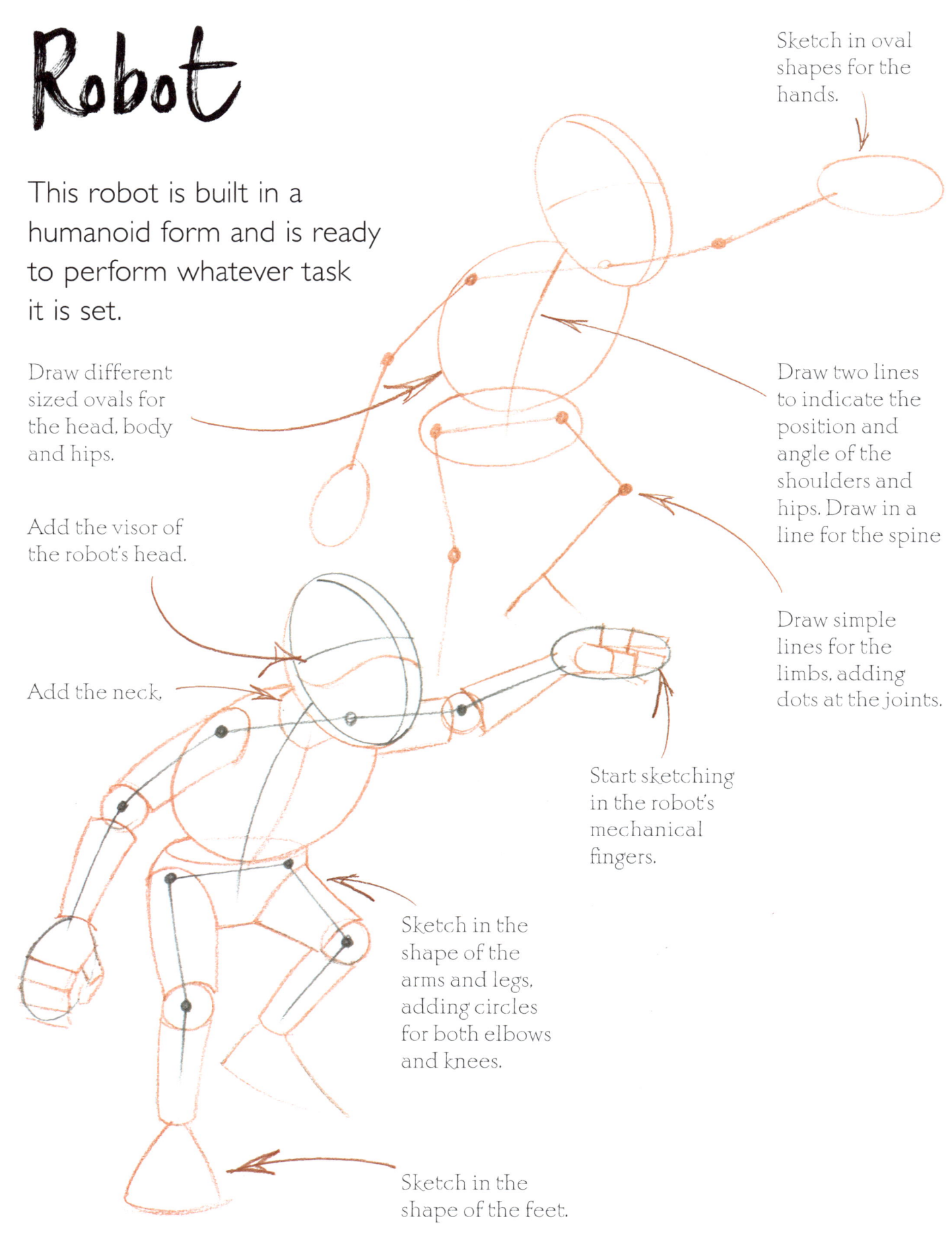

24

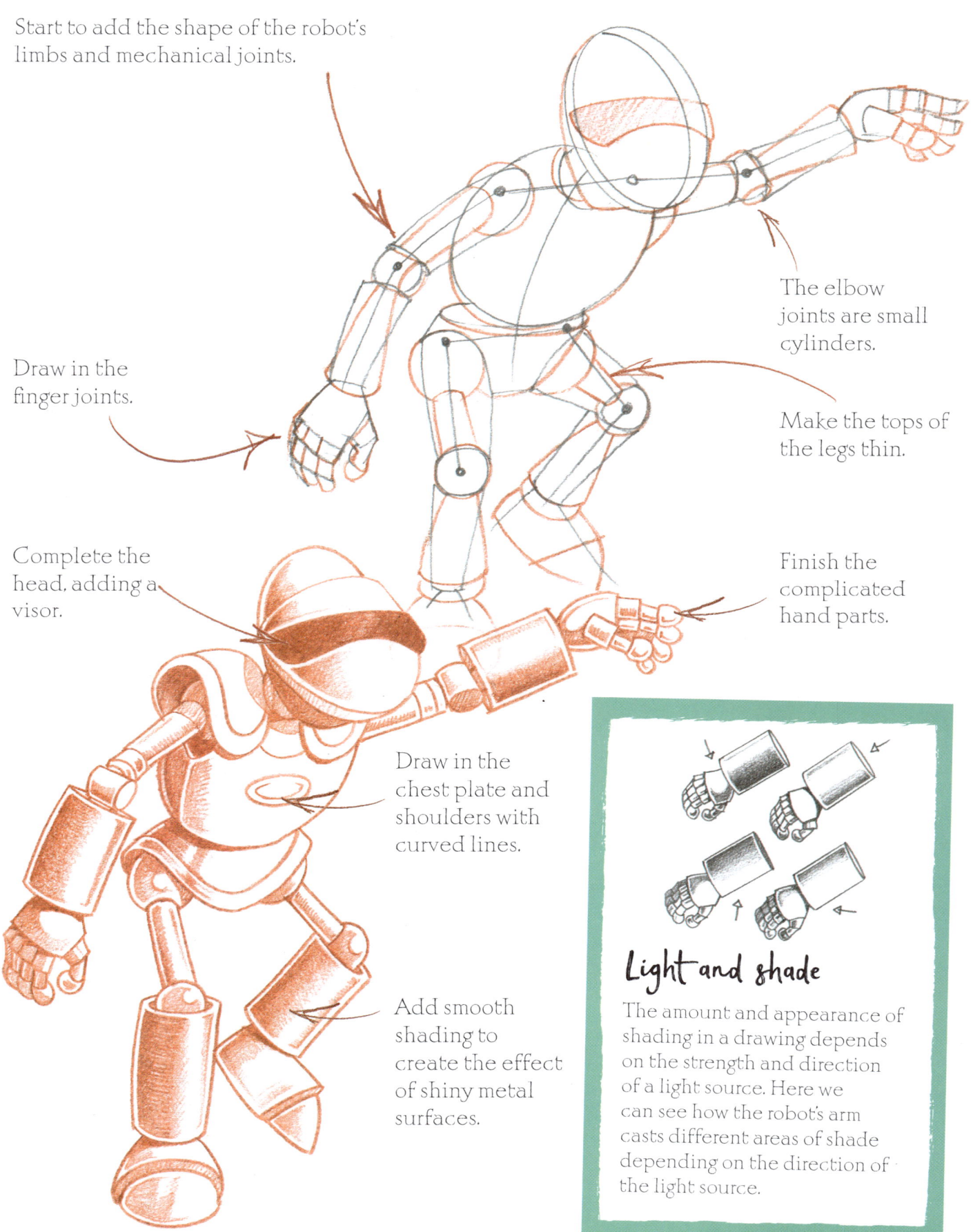

Start to add the shape of the robot's limbs and mechanical joints.

The elbow joints are small cylinders.

Draw in the finger joints.

Make the tops of the legs thin.

Complete the head, adding a visor.

Finish the complicated hand parts.

Draw in the chest plate and shoulders with curved lines.

Add smooth shading to create the effect of shiny metal surfaces.

Light and shade

The amount and appearance of shading in a drawing depends on the strength and direction of a light source. Here we can see how the robot's arm casts different areas of shade depending on the direction of the light source.

25

Kimono girl

This girl is in a kneeling position and is dressed in a traditional oriental kimono. The draped folds of the costume can be challenging to draw.

Draw different sized ovals, for the head, body and hips.

Draw two lines to indicate the position and angle of the shoulders and hips. Draw in a line for the spine.

As the figure is kneeling you only have to position the upper legs.

Position the facial features in the lower half of the head.

Sketch one hand going behind the head.

Add both arms using the construction lines as a guide.

Add dots to position the joints.

Place this hand on the figure's lap.

26

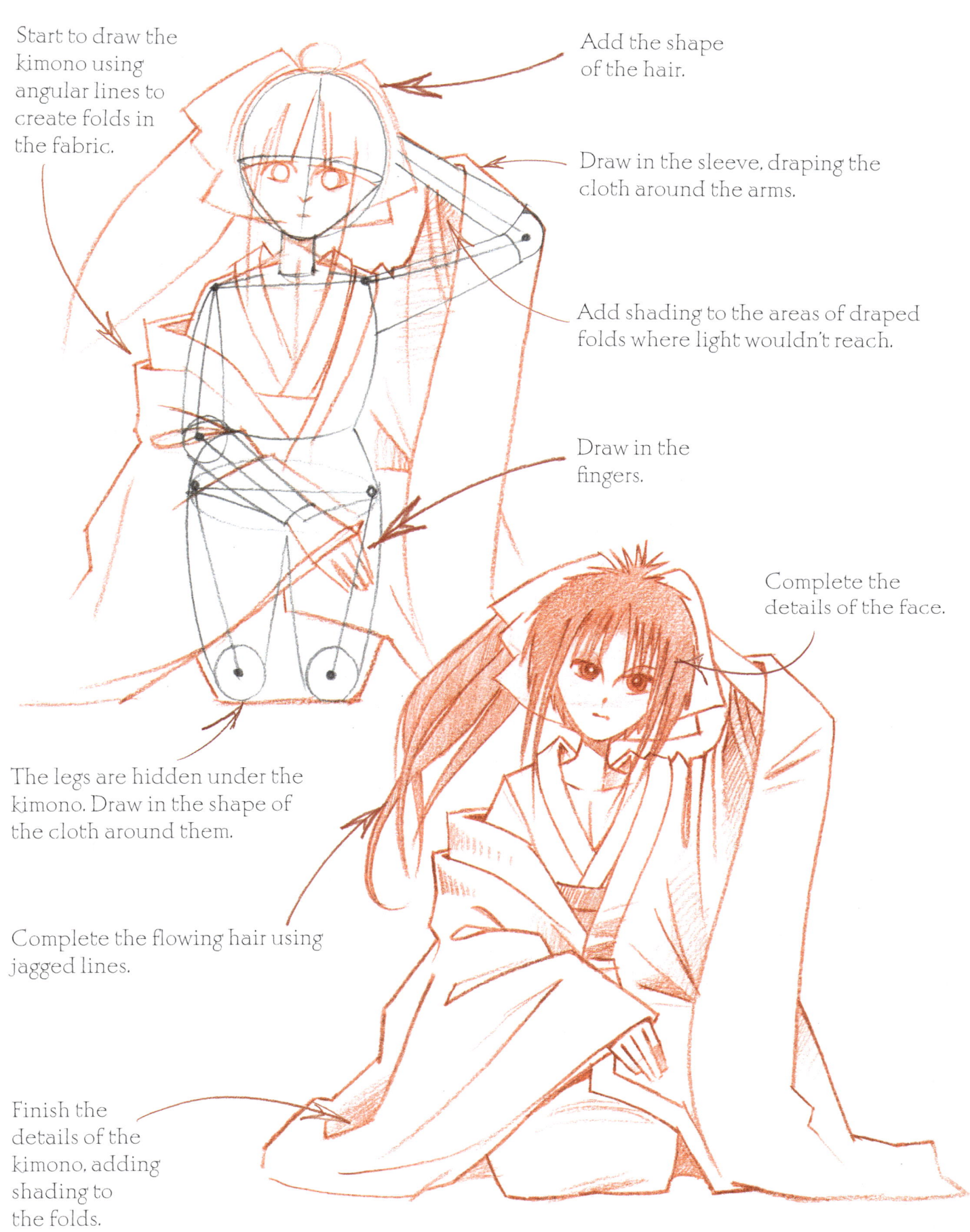

Explosive action!

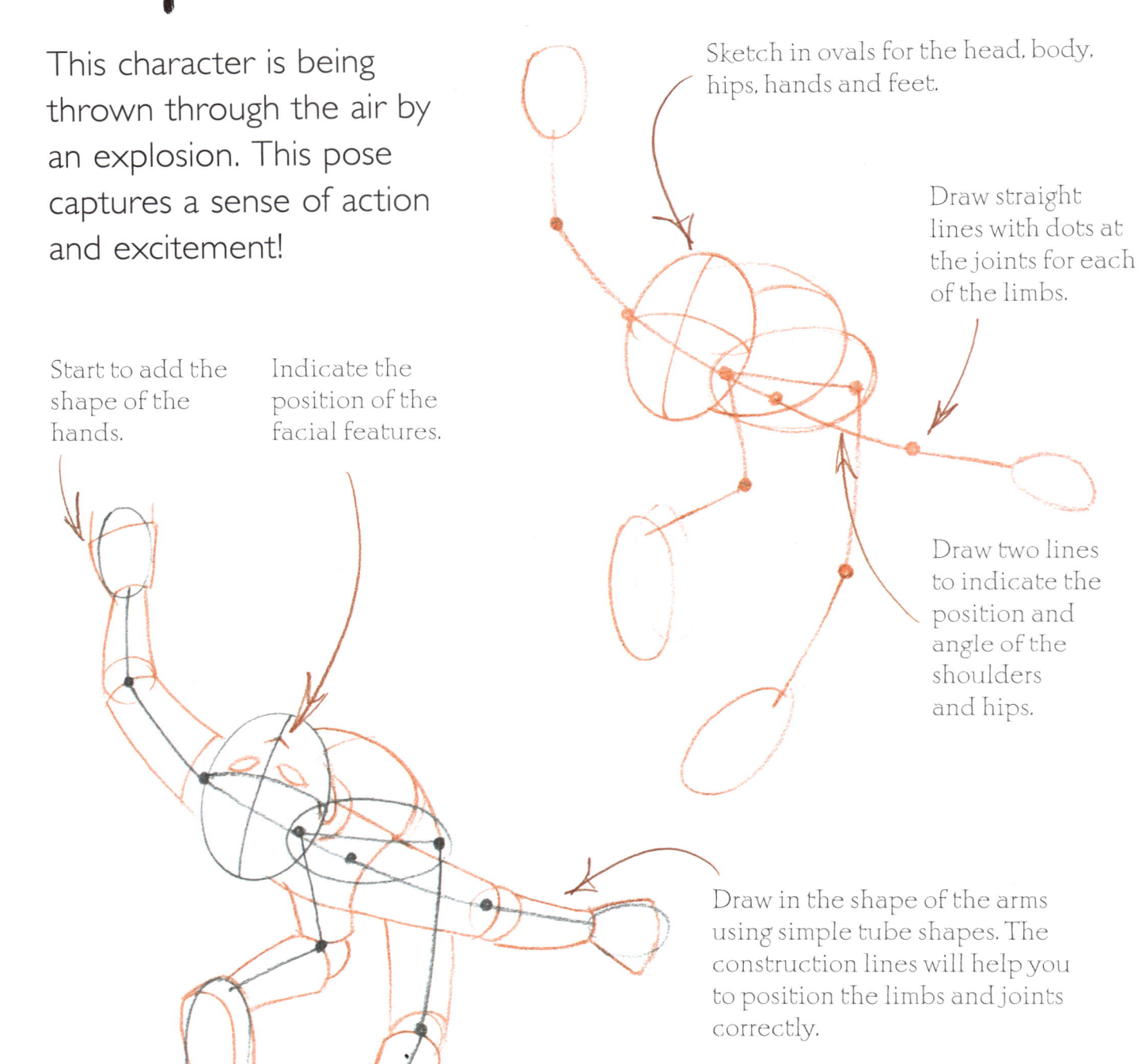

This character is being thrown through the air by an explosion. This pose captures a sense of action and excitement!

Sketch in ovals for the head, body, hips, hands and feet.

Draw straight lines with dots at the joints for each of the limbs.

Draw two lines to indicate the position and angle of the shoulders and hips.

Start to add the shape of the hands.

Indicate the position of the facial features.

Draw in the shape of the arms using simple tube shapes. The construction lines will help you to position the limbs and joints correctly.

Add the shape of the legs using simple tube shapes. The legs are different sizes due to the exaggerated pose and perspective.

Add more detail to the shape of the feet.

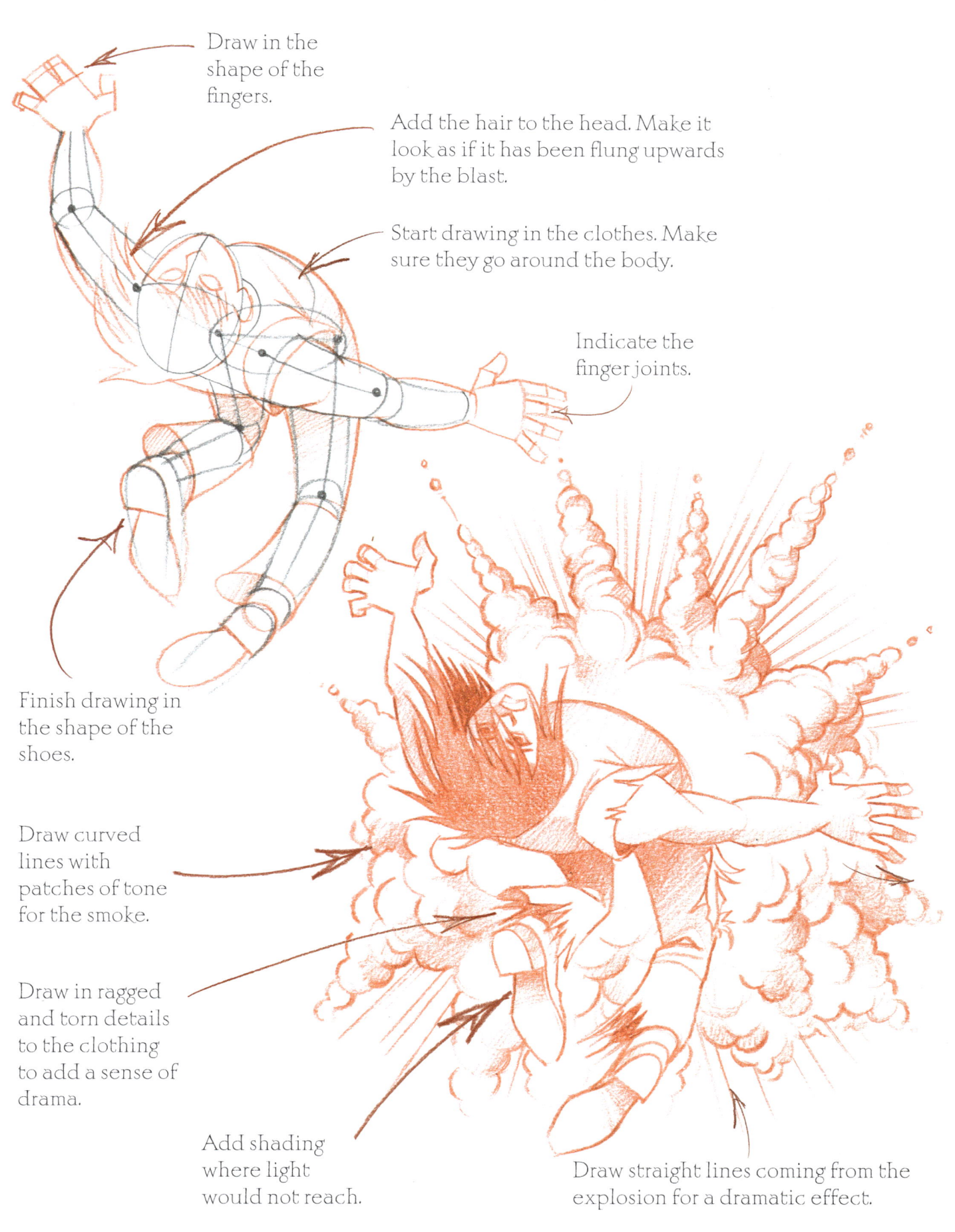

Robo-tortoise and girl

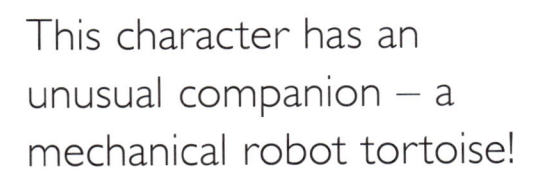

This character has an unusual companion – a mechanical robot tortoise!

First draw in the main shapes of the figure and the tortoise.

Draw ovals for the body, head and hips. Add straight lines for the limbs.

Sketch in the shape of the girl's hair, with the fringe ending just above her eyes.

Mark the position of the facial features.

Draw in the shapes of the girl's body, using the construction lines as a guide.

Draw a large oval for the tortoise's body and a small oval for its head.

Draw in the tortoise's shell. Add two curved lines to create the shape of the shell.

Add in the neck.

Add the back legs of the tortoise.

30

Glossary

Composition The positioning of a picture on the drawing paper.

Construction lines Guidelines used in the early stages of a drawing which are usually erased later.

Cross-hatching A series of criss-crossing lines used to add shade to a drawing.

Fixative A type of resin used to spray over a finished drawing to prevent smudging. It should only be used by an adult.

Hatching A series of parallel lines used to add shade to a drawing.

Light source The direction from which the light seems to come in a drawing.

Profile A view from the side, especially a side view of a person's head or face.

Reference Photographs or other images used to help produce a drawing, if drawing from life is not possible.

Silhouette A drawing that shows only a dark shape, like a shadow.

Three-dimensional Having an effect of depth, so as to look lifelike or real.

Vanishing point The place in a perspective drawing where parallel lines appear to meet.

Index

B
brushes 7

C
charcoal 6, 8
construction lines 13-14, 19-23, 25-31
crayons 6, 8
cross-hatching 9

D
drawing feet 18
drawing tools 6-7
dynamic backgrounds 21

E
explosive action 28-29
expressions 14-15

F
felt-tips 8, 9
finger painting 6
fixative 6

H
hair 16-17
hatching 9, 31
heads 12-13

K
kimono 26-27
kneeling girl 26-27

L
light and shade 25

M
making a start 4-5
martial arts 20
materials 8-9
mirror 14

P
pencils 6-9
pens 7-9
perspective 10-11
profile 12

R
robo-tortoise and girl 30-31
robot 24-25

S
samurai 18-19
silhouette 8
sketchbook 4
sword 18-19

V
vanishing points 10-11

W
warrior 22-23
watercolour pencils 6